THE BEST NFL
DEFENSES
OF ALL TIME

By Will Graves

Published by ABDO Publishing Company, PO Box 398166, Minneapolis, MN 55439. Copyright © 2014 by Abdo Consulting Group, Inc. International copyrights reserved in all countries. No part of this book may be reproduced in any form without written permission from the publisher. SportsZone™ is a trademark and logo of ABDO Publishing Company.

Printed in the United States of America,
North Mankato, Minnesota
052013
012014

Editor: Chrös McDougall
Series Designer: Christa Schneider

Photo Credits: NFL Photos/AP Images, cover (left), 1 (left), 9, 15, 17, 19, 23, 27, 31; Four Seam Images via AP Images, cover (right), 1 (right), 53; AP Images, 7, 11, 25, 29, 35, 43; Charles Kelly/AP Images, 13; Rich Clarkson Associates via AP Images, 21; George Gojkovich/Getty Images, 33; Pete Leabo/AP Images, 37; Paul Spinelli/AP Images, 39; Eric Risberg/AP Images, 41; Lennox McLendon/AP Images, 45; Amy Sancetta/AP Images, 47; Susan Ragan/AP Images, 49; Mark Humphrey/AP Images, 51; Al Behrman/AP Images, 55; Chris O'Meara/AP Images, 57; Scott Boehm/AP Images, 59; Winslow Townson/AP Images, 61

Library of Congress Control Number: 2013931958

Cataloging-in-Publication Data
Graves, Will.
 The best NFL defenses of all time / Will Graves.
   p. cm. -- (NFL's best ever)
Includes bibliographical references and index.
ISBN 978-1-61783-907-8
1. National Football League--Juvenile literature. 2. Defense (Football)--Juvenile literature. I. Title.
796.332--dc23

                                        2013931958

TABLE OF CONTENTS

INTRODUCTION

You don't need a great nickname to have a great defense. But sometimes it helps.

Some of the best defenses in National Football League (NFL) history have had colorful nicknames, such as the "Steel Curtain," the "Fearsome Foursome," and the "Purple People Eaters." Teams didn't need a nickname to dominate, though. Throughout the years the best defenses have featured furious pass rushers, smart and nimble linebackers, and fast, hard-hitting defensive backs. Most importantly, these defenses have helped their teams win.

Here are some of the best defenses in NFL history.

1942
CHICAGO
BEARS

Many players during the 1930s and 1940s played both offense and defense. Clyde "Bulldog" Turner was one of them. He was an All-Pro at center seven times during his career. But it was his work at linebacker that turned his Chicago Bears into the "Monsters of the Midway."

These days NFL teams rely on videos to scout opponents. Turner was one of the first to use that practice. He would study game film using a projector and a movie screen. He said he wanted to know where every player on defense needed to be during a play.

Turner's studying showed on the field. Opposing offenses never seemed to know where he was. That was especially true in 1942. He led the NFL with eight interceptions that season. His effort helped anchor one of the most dominant defenses in league history.

Danny Fortmann played guard and linebacker for the 1942 Chicago Bears.

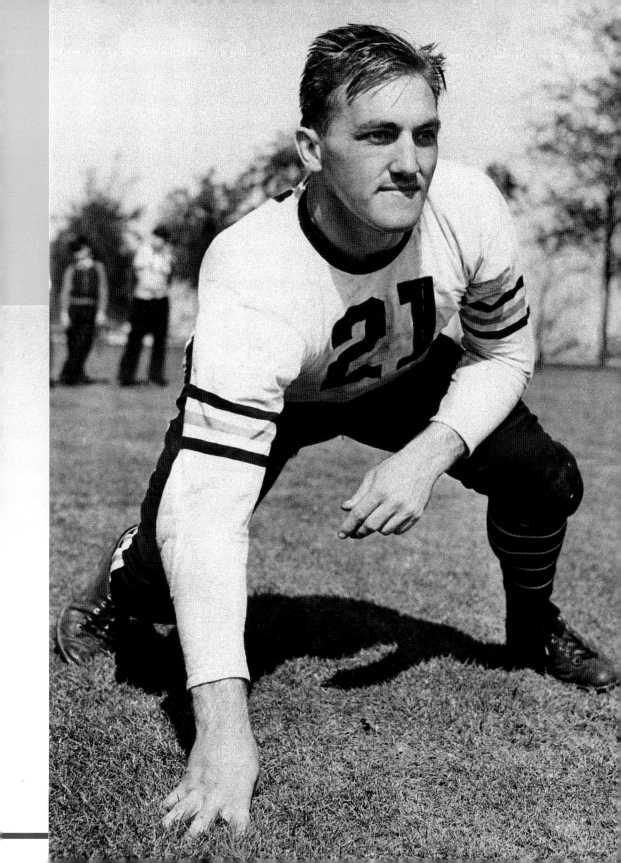

The 1942 Bears went 11–0 in the regular season. They won four of those games by shutout. And they allowed just one touchdown in four others. Passing was rare in pro football at the time. Yet the Bears gave up just 519 rushing yards all season. No team had allowed fewer rushing yards through 2012.

The Bears were heavy favorites to win the NFL Championship Game (the Super Bowl did not begin until 1967). Their perfect season, however, didn't end perfectly. The Washington Redskins upset them in the title game, 14–6. Chicago's defense scored the Bears' only touchdown of the game on a fumble return. But the Redskins rushed for 104 yards. It tied for the most rushing yards Chicago gave up all season.

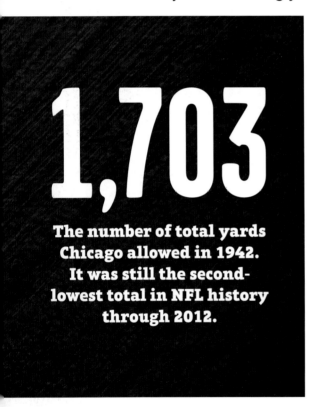

1,703

The number of total yards Chicago allowed in 1942. It was still the second-lowest total in NFL history through 2012.

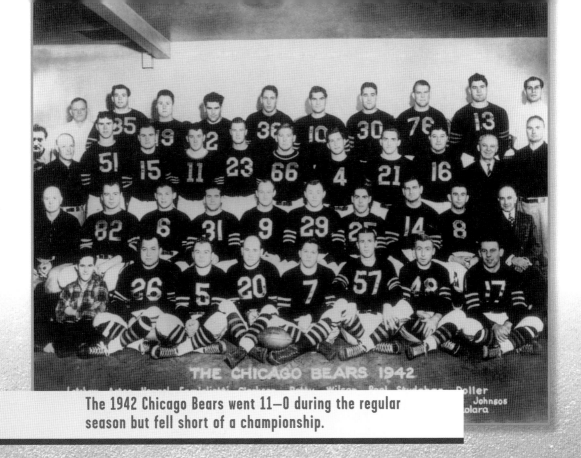

THE CHICAGO BEARS 1942

The 1942 Chicago Bears went 11–0 during the regular season but fell short of a championship.

1942 CHICAGO BEARS
KEY STATS AND PLAYERS

Record: 11–0

Postseason: Lost the NFL Championship Game 14–6 to Washington Redskins

Danny Fortmann
Positions: Guard/Linebacker
Age: 26
College: Colgate University

Sid Luckman
Positions: Quarterback/Cornerback
Age: 26
College: Columbia University

Clyde "Bulldog" Turner
Positions: Center/Linebacker
Age: 23
College: Hardin-Simmons University

George Wilson
Position: Defensive End
Age: 28
College: Northwestern University

1962
GREEN BAY
PACKERS

Off the field, Ray Nitschke's teammates said the linebacker could be the nicest person on the planet. Put him in a helmet and pads, though, and look out. The hard-hitting linebacker was the heartbeat of the Green Bay Packers' defense during the 1960s. He didn't just tackle opponents. He tried to grind them into the turf.

The Packers were strong in nearly every season of Nitschke's 15-year career. Green Bay was crowned champion five times in the 1960s. However, the team was at its best in 1962. Legendary coach Vince Lombardi was in charge. Green Bay's defense featured five future Hall of Fame players, including Nitschke. And the Packers rolled to their second straight NFL title.

Ray Nitschke led the 1962 Green Bay Packers to an NFL championship.

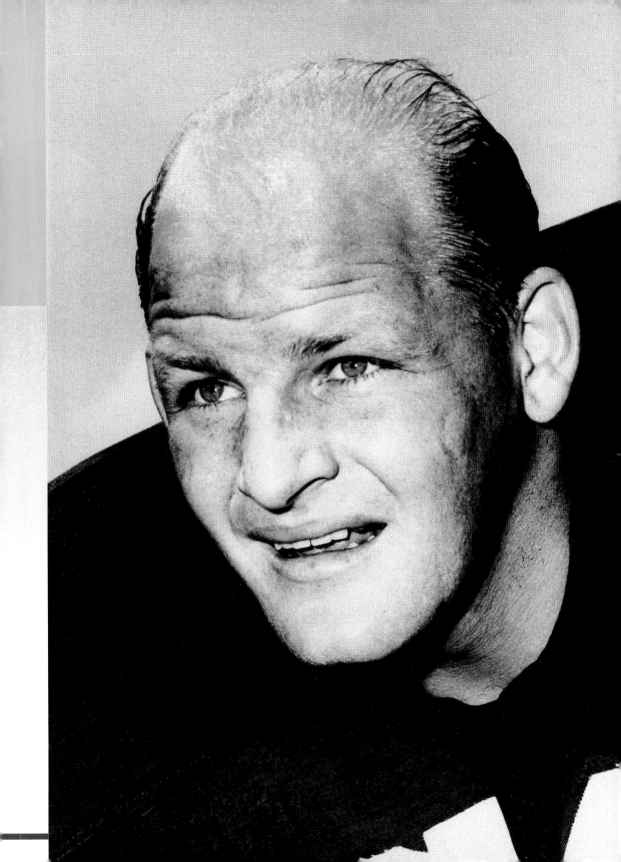

Green Bay led the NFL with the fewest points allowed that season.

Plus the team created an amazing 50 turnovers in just 14 games. Green Bay's defense forced opposing offenses to make a tough choice on every play. They could choose to run. But they'd have to get past Nitschke and defensive linemen Henry Jordan and Willie Davis if they did. They also could choose to pass. But that risked safety Willie Wood or cornerback Herb Adderley picking off the ball.

Moving the ball against the Packers proved almost impossible. The New York Giants certainly struggled to do so in the NFL title game. It was a bitter cold day at Yankee Stadium. That was perfect weather for one of the toughest defenses ever to play. And New York's offense never reached the end zone in a 16–7 loss.

452

The number of interception return yards by the Packers in 1962. Cornerback Herb Adderley and safety Willie Wood each had 132.

Green Bay Packers Willie Wood (24) and Hank Gremminger
(46) take down a Baltimore Colts player in a 1962 game.

1962 GREEN BAY PACKERS
KEY STATS AND PLAYERS

Record: 13–1

Postseason: Won the NFL Championship Game 16–7 over the New
York Giants

Herb Adderley
Position: Cornerback
Age: 23
College: Michigan State University

Ray Nitschke
Position: Linebacker
Age: 26
College: University of Illinois

Willie Davis
Position: Defensive End
Age: 28
College: Grambling State
University

Willie Wood
Position: Safety
Age: 26
College: University of Southern
California

1967
LOS ANGELES RAMS

Los Angeles Rams players Deacon Jones, Lamar Lundy, Merlin Olsen, and Rosey Grier weren't the first defensive line to be called the "Fearsome Foursome." The New York Giants and the San Diego Chargers both had the nickname thrown around during the 1950s and 1960s. But when the Rams' line was done chasing after quarterbacks, they'd retired the nickname for good.

The Rams were doormats for much of the 1960s. They often finished at the back of the pack. But things changed when coach George Allen arrived in 1966. He let his defensive front four loose in a way that helped change the game for good. The term "sack" didn't exist until Jones began using it. It described a play where he tackled a quarterback trying to throw.

Los Angeles Rams defensive end Lamar Lundy was a terror for opposing offensive lines.

Jones, Lundy, Olsen, and Grier were the Rams' original Fearsome Foursome. Roger Brown replaced Grier in 1967. That year the woeful Rams became one of the best teams in football. Los Angeles went 11–1–2. It made it to the playoffs for the first time in 12 years. And Jones, Brown, and Olsen all made the Pro Bowl. But the Fearsome Foursome didn't do it alone.

Linebacker Jack Pardee and cornerback Eddie Meador were star pass defenders. They combined for 14 interceptions. That helped the Rams' defense lead the NFL in fewest points allowed. But all those sacks didn't lead to a title. The powerful Green Bay Packers beat the Rams 28–7 in the playoffs.

26

The unofficial number of sacks by Jones in 1967. That total would be a record, but sacks didn't become an official NFL statistic until 1982.

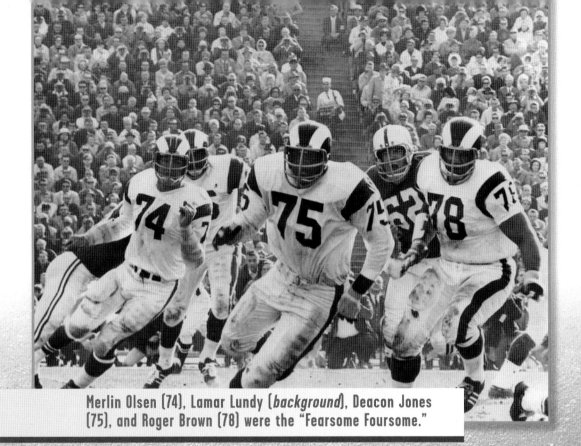

Merlin Olsen (74), Lamar Lundy (*background*), Deacon Jones (75), and Roger Brown (78) were the "Fearsome Foursome."

1967 LOS ANGELES RAMS
KEY STATS AND PLAYERS

Record: 11–1–2

Postseason: Lost in the playoffs 28–7 to the Green Bay Packers

Roger Brown
Position: Defensive Tackle
Age: 30
College: University of Maryland-Eastern Shore

David "Deacon" Jones
Position: Defensive End
Age: 29
College: Mississippi Valley State University

Lamar Lundy
Position: Defensive End
Age: 32
College: Purdue University

Merlin Olsen
Position: Defensive Tackle
Age: 27
College: Utah State University

1969
KANSAS CITY
CHIEFS

The lowest moment of the Kansas City Chiefs' 1966 season led to one of the best decisions in team history. The Green Bay Packers had whipped the Chiefs 35–10 in Super Bowl I after the 1966 season. So Chiefs coach Hank Stram went looking for help on defense. He ended up taking linebacker Willie Lanier in the second round of the 1967 draft.

Lanier's teammates called him "Contact," because he hit opposing players so hard. An equipment manager sometimes put padding on the outside of Lanier's helmet. It softened the blow so he would not hurt himself when crushing into opponents.

The Chiefs' defense already included stars such as defensive lineman Buck Buchanan, linebacker Bobby Bell, and cornerback Emmitt Thomas. But Lanier's big hits proved to be the missing piece.

Kansas City Chiefs linebacker Willie Lanier (63) drops back into pass coverage during a 1969 game.

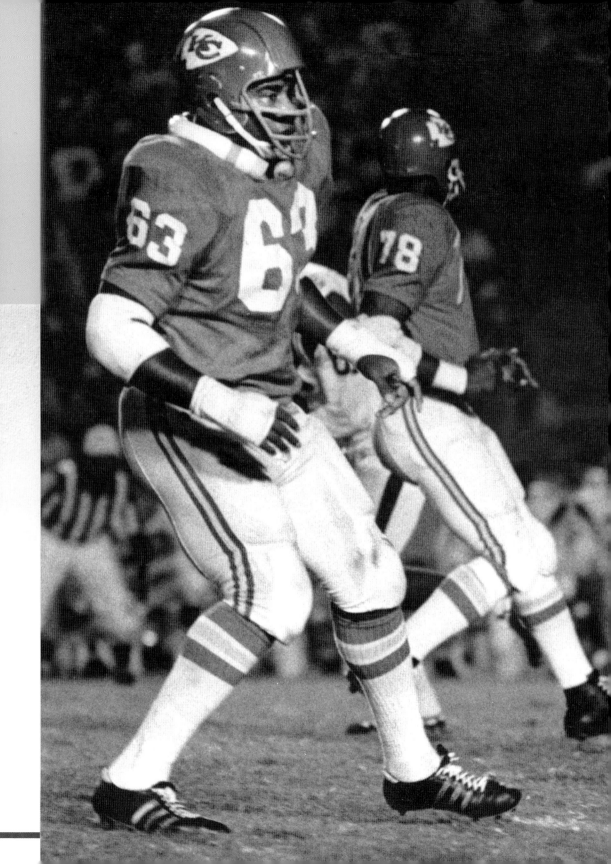

All four players later ended up in the Hall of Fame. And they proved to be a big part of one of the most important wins in football history.

Kansas City was back in the Super Bowl after the 1969 season. This time they faced the mighty Minnesota Vikings in Super Bowl IV. The Chiefs were heavy underdogs. Yet they pulled off a 23–7 upset. The defense forced five turnovers. Lanier got one of Kansas City's three interceptions.

The win gave the American Football League (AFL) its second straight Super Bowl win. The AFL would merge with the NFL the next season. Kansas City's victory helped prove AFL teams could compete with teams in the NFL.

13

The number of turnovers created by the 1969 Chiefs in three playoff wins.

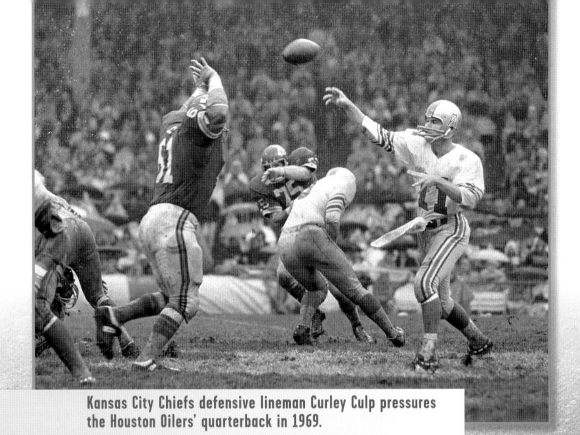

Kansas City Chiefs defensive lineman Curley Culp pressures the Houston Oilers' quarterback in 1969.

1969 KANSAS CITY CHIEFS

KEY STATS AND PLAYERS

Record: 11–3

Postseason: Won Super Bowl IV 23–7 over the Minnesota Vikings

Bobby Bell

Position: Linebacker

Age: 29

College: University of Minnesota

Willie Lanier

Position: Linebacker

Age: 24

College: Morgan State University

Buck Buchanan

Position: Defensive Tackle

Age: 29

College: Grambling State University

Emmitt Thomas

Position: Cornerback

Age: 26

College: Bishop College

1970
MINNESOTA VIKINGS

They were called the "Purple People Eaters." Carl Eller. Alan Page. Jim Marshall. Gary Larsen. Alone, the four Minnesota Viking defensive linemen were dangerous. Together, they were nearly unstoppable.

The quartet would tell each other in the huddle that they would "meet at the quarterback." And oftentimes they did just that. The Vikings didn't just beat teams during the early 1970s. They overwhelmed them. Eller, Page, Marshall, and Larsen swarmed the field in their purple jerseys. They earned their colorful nickname for the way they ate up opponents.

Minnesota certainly feasted in 1970. The Vikings' offense often struggled to move the ball. Yet the team went 12–2 that season. The Vikings led the NFL in fewest yards allowed for the second straight year.

From left, Jim Marshall, Carl Eller, Alan Page, and Gary Larsen were the "Purple People Eaters."

The Purple People Eaters were a perfect combination of size and speed. Marshall and Eller would race by offensive tackles. Meanwhile Page and Larsen would clog up the middle with their strength. The combination left opponents with nowhere to go.

Page had a nose for the ball. He recovered seven fumbles in 1970. He returned one for a touchdown. Eller, Larsen, and Marshall each had two fumble recoveries. All that ball-hawking helped the Vikings roll to the playoffs.

The Purple People Eaters couldn't lift the Vikings to the Super Bowl, though. Minnesota lost to the San Francisco 49ers in the playoffs. Losing in the postseason became a habit for the Vikings. Minnesota reached the Super Bowl four times in the 1970s and lost all four.

8

The number of games in which the Vikings held opponents to less than 70 rushing yards in 1970. Minnesota was 8–0 in those games.

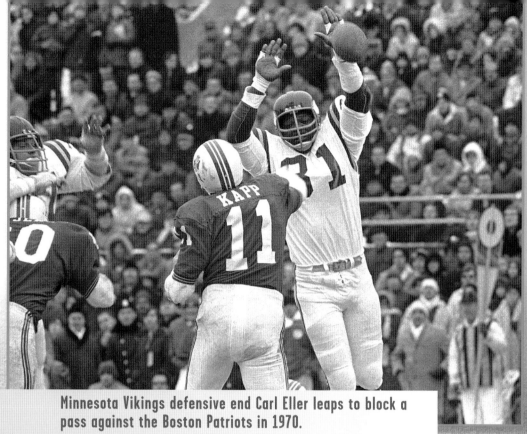

Minnesota Vikings defensive end Carl Eller leaps to block a pass against the Boston Patriots in 1970.

1970 MINNESOTA VIKINGS
KEY STATS AND PLAYERS

Record: 12–2

Postseason: Lost in the playoffs 17–14 to the San Francisco 49ers

Carl Eller
Position: Defensive End
Age: 28
College: University of Minnesota

Jim Marshall
Position: Defensive End
Age: 33
College: Ohio State University

Gary Larsen
Position: Defensive Tackle
Age: 30
College: Concordia College (Illinois)

Alan Page
Position: Defensive Tackle
Age: 25
College: University of Notre Dame

1972 MIAMI DOLPHINS

There weren't a lot of stars on the Miami Dolphins defense in the early 1970s. The headlines went to the players on offense. Players such as quarterback Bob Griese and running backs Larry Csonka and Mercury Morris were the stars.

That was fine by linebacker Nick Buoniconti. He figured the offense could get all the attention as long as the defense did its job. And no defense in the history of the league did its job better than the 1972 Dolphins. Miami went a perfect 17–0 that season. Through 2012 that Dolphins squad remained the only unbeaten team in the Super Bowl era.

Miami Dolphins defensive end Manny Fernandez tackles a Washington Redskins ball carrier during Super Bowl VII.

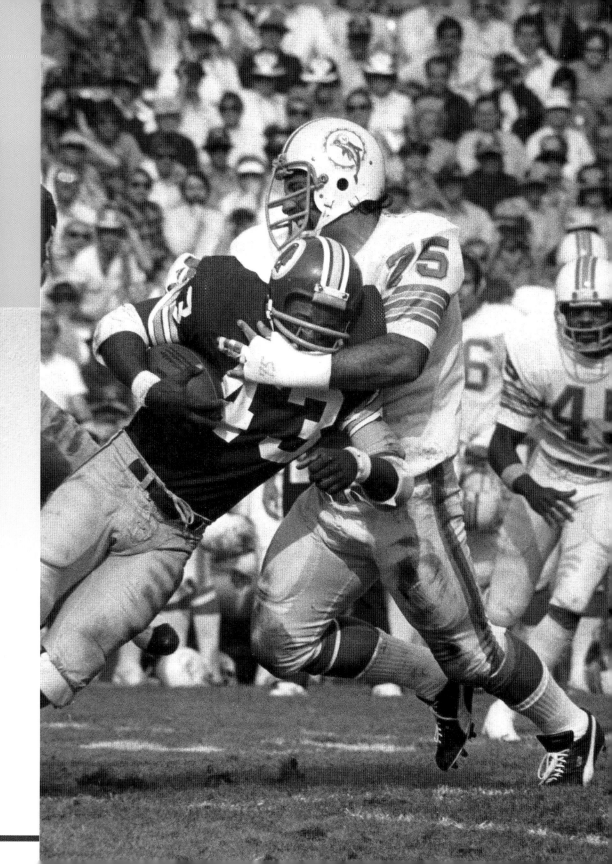

Miami's offense was dealt a blow when Griese broke his leg. That forced him to miss most of the season. But the "No-Name Defense" made sure that was not a problem. Players such as defensive tackle Manny Fernandez and safety Jake Scott stepped up. Most of the games weren't even close. The offense would wear down teams with Csonka and Morris. That gave the defense plenty of time to rest on the sideline. When the defense came in, it would quickly shut down the other team.

26

The number of interceptions made by the Dolphins during the 1972 regular season. Meanwhile, Miami gave up just 10 touchdown passes all season.

Miami won 11 of its 14 regular-season games by at least 10 points. The defense led the league in fewest yards and points allowed. The "No Names" capped off their great season in Super Bowl VII against the Washington Redskins. Scott picked off two passes to earn the Most Valuable Player (MVP) Award in a 14–7 victory.

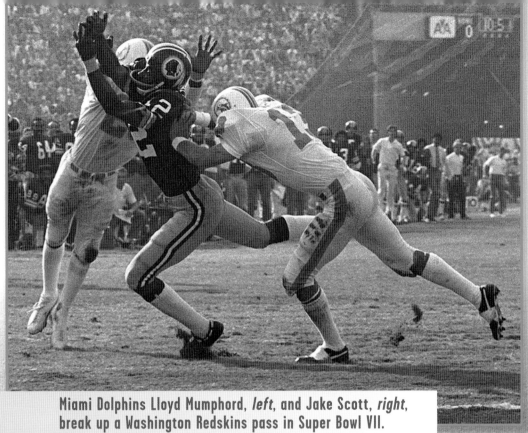

Miami Dolphins Lloyd Mumphord, *left*, and Jake Scott, *right*, break up a Washington Redskins pass in Super Bowl VII.

1972 MIAMI DOLPHINS
KEY STATS AND PLAYERS

Record: 14–0

Postseason: Won Super Bowl VII 14–7 over the Washington Redskins

---

Dick Anderson

Position: Safety

Age: 26

College: University of Colorado

Manny Fernandez

Position: Defensive tackle

Age: 26

College: University of Utah

Nick Buoniconti

Position: Linebacker

Age: 32

College: University of Notre Dame

Jake Scott

Position: Safety

Age: 27

College: University of Georgia

1976
PITTSBURGH STEELERS

The Pittsburgh Steelers went into the 1976 season in search of a third straight Super Bowl win. But they got off to just a 1–4 start. Injuries began piling up, too. Quarterback Terry Bradshaw and wide receivers Lynn Swann and John Stallworth missed several games. That made points hard to come by. Winning another Super Bowl became an afterthought. The Steelers now had to worry about just making the playoffs.

That's when the "Steel Curtain" defense took over.

A trio of Hall of Fame players led the way. Defensive tackle "Mean" Joe Greene and linebackers Jack Lambert and Jack Ham led the Steelers to nine straight wins. Getting into the end zone against Pittsburgh's "Steel Curtain" defense was almost impossible during that stretch.

"Mean" Joe Greene was the anchor of the Pittsburgh Steelers' defensive line during the 1970s.

The Steelers posted five shutouts and allowed only two total touchdowns in those games. At one point opponents went more than six weeks without scoring an offensive touchdown.

Pittsburgh set a record by allowing just 138

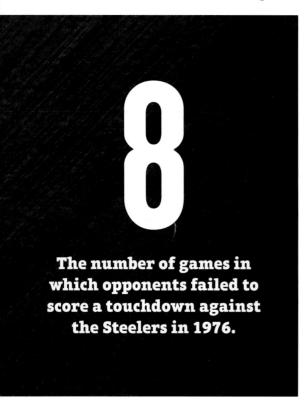

8

The number of games in which opponents failed to score a touchdown against the Steelers in 1976.

points the whole season. That was fewer than 10 points per game. Eight defensive starters made the Pro Bowl. Meanwhile, the Steelers rallied to post a 10–4 record. That was good enough to claim their fifth straight playoff berth.

A third straight Super Bowl was still out of reach, though. Pittsburgh's season ended with a 24–7 loss to the Oakland Raiders in the conference championship game. It was one of the few setbacks during a decade of dominance by the Steelers. Pittsburgh returned to the top after the 1978 and 1979 seasons. The team won back-to-back Super Bowls in large part thanks to the Steel Curtain defense.

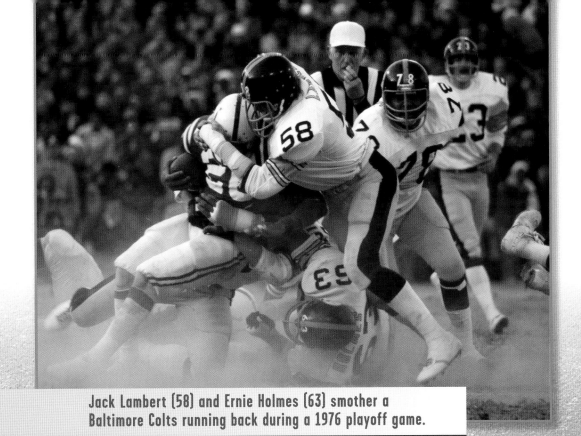

Jack Lambert (58) and Ernie Holmes (63) smother a
Baltimore Colts running back during a 1976 playoff game.

1976 PITTSBURGH STEELERS
KEY STATS AND PLAYERS

Record: 10–4

Postseason: Lost in the conference championship game 24–7 to the
Oakland Raiders

Mel Blount
Position: Cornerback
Age: 28
College: Southern University

"Mean" Joe Greene
Position: Defensive Tackle
Age: 30
College: University of North Texas

L. C. Greenwood
Position: Defensive End
Age: 30
College: University of Arkansas at
Pine Bluff

Jack Lambert
Position: Linebacker
Age: 24
College: Kent State University

1977
DALLAS COWBOYS

"Doomsday Defense" sounds like something out of a science fiction movie. On the field, however, it looked more like a horror movie for the Dallas Cowboys' opponents in the 1970s.

Defensive linemen Randy White and Ed "Too Tall" Jones led the powerful unit. And the Doomsday Defense was never more powerful than in 1977. That year Dallas broke through to win its second Super Bowl title.

White actually spent the first two seasons of his career at linebacker. Coach Tom Landry moved him to the line in 1977. White's quickness made him a tough matchup for bigger, slower offensive lineman. Linemen would surge forward to move White out of the way. Then White would slip past and into the backfield to make a play.

Dallas Cowboys defensive end Harvey Martin jumps to sack the Washington Redskins' quarterback in 1977.

While White was quick, Jones really was "Too Tall." At 6 feet, 9 inches, Jones would reach up his arms and knock down passes. At least, that's what he would do when he wasn't wrapping up quarterbacks.

Jones and White were quiet leaders. Linebacker Thomas "Hollywood" Henderson did all the talking. Henderson's play sometimes couldn't keep up with his mouth. But he made an impact in 1977 as the Cowboys rolled to a championship.

The Doomsday Defense shined in Super Bowl XII. It forced eight turnovers in a 27–10 win over the Denver Broncos. White and defensive end Harvey Martin shared MVP honors in the game. That's because the NFL wouldn't let the entire 11-man defense share the award.

8

The number of turnovers the Cowboys forced in Super Bowl XII, a record until the Cowboys forced nine in Super Bowl XXVII.

Dallas Cowboys safety Cliff Harris (43) tackles a Miami
Dolphins wide receiver during a 1977 game.

1977 DALLAS COWBOYS
KEY STATS AND PLAYERS

Record: 12–2

Postseason: Won Super Bowl XII 27–10 over the Denver Broncos

Thomas "Hollywood" Henderson
Position: Linebacker
Age: 24
College: Langston University

Ed "Too Tall" Jones
Position: Defensive End
Age: 26
College: Tennessee State University

Harvey Martin
Position: Defensive End
Age: 27
College: Texas A&M University-Commerce

Randy White
Position: Defensive Tackle
Age: 24
College: University of Maryland

1984
SAN FRANCISCO
49ERS

It could get pretty lonely playing in quarterback Joe Montana's shadow.

Yet the guys on the San Francisco 49ers' defense spent most of the 1980s doing just that. Montana was the face of the 49ers' run to four Super Bowls in the decade. But the defense made sure it was not forgotten in one memorable Super Bowl performance.

The 49ers rolled through 1984 like a racecar on cruise control. The NFL regular season had jumped to 16 games from 14 games in 1978. The 1984 team became the first to win 15 games in one season. Then it had little trouble advancing through the playoffs to the Super Bowl.

San Francisco 49ers safety Dwight Hicks waits for the snap during a 1984 playoff game against the New York Giants.

That's where the team was supposed to run into big trouble. The Miami Dolphins set records of their own that season behind quarterback Dan Marino. He had torched the league for 48 touchdown passes. Most people expected Super Bowl XIX to be an offensive show.

There was a show all right. Only it was put on by the San Francisco defense. Future Hall of Famer Ronnie Lott led the 49ers in a 38–16 rout. The Dolphins barely even tried running the ball. They rushed just nine times for 25 yards. Instead they put their hopes on Marino's arm. He indeed passed for 318 yards. But the 49ers picked off two of his passes in the second half.

The 49ers would go on to become the NFL's dominant dynasty of the 1980s. Montana got much of the credit. But as the defense showed in 1984, it was not just along for the ride.

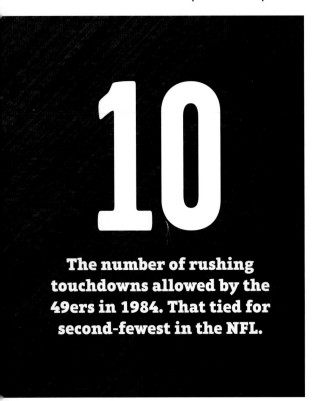

10

The number of rushing touchdowns allowed by the 49ers in 1984. That tied for second-fewest in the NFL.

San Francisco 49ers defenders smother a New York Giants ball carrier during a 1984 playoff game.

1984 SAN FRANCISCO 49ERS

KEY STATS AND PLAYERS

Record: 15–1

Postseason: Won Super Bowl XIX 38–16 over the Miami Dolphins

Dwaine Board

Position: Defensive End

Age: 28

College: North Carolina A&T State University

Ronnie Lott

Position: Cornerback

Age: 25

College: University of Southern California

Keena Turner

Position: Linebacker

Age: 26

College: Purdue University

Eric Wright

Position: Cornerback

Age: 25

College: University of Missouri

1985
CHICAGO
BEARS

The Chicago Bears made a music video at the start of the 1985 season called "The Super Bowl Shuffle." Then their prediction came true. Only, the Bears didn't "shuffle" to a Super Bowl win. They stomped their way to it.

The defense, as it always does in Chicago, led the way. Defensive coordinator Buddy Ryan came up with a new defense he called the "46" defense. The name came from safety Doug Plank's No. 46 jersey. Ryan would bring Plank close to the line of scrimmage to blitz the quarterback. The Bears blitzed better than anybody. They collected 64 sacks that season. Defensive ends Richard Dent and Dan Hampton as well as middle linebacker Mike Singletary also were keys on the blitz.

Chicago Bears linebacker Mike Singletary runs upfield to make a tackle during the 1985 season.

Chicago allowed the fewest points in the league. And the team only got better as the season went on. The Bears won two playoff games in shutouts. That brought them to their first Super Bowl. Super Bowl XX against the New England Patriots proved to be a mismatch.

Chicago won 46–10. The Bears forced New England into six turnovers. Dent won the game's MVP award after collecting 1.5 sacks and forcing two fumbles.

The Bears' defense was so good in 1985 that nose tackle William "The Refrigerator" Perry had time to play on offense, too. The 325-pound big man became a touchdown-scoring fullback that season. He even scored an offensive touchdown in the Super Bowl. The defensive players celebrated the win by carrying Ryan off the field on their shoulders.

+23

The 1985 Bears' turnover ratio, the best in the NFL.

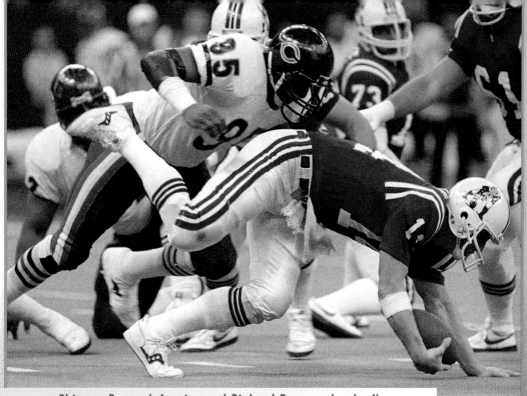

Chicago Bears defensive end Richard Dent sacks the New England Patriots' quarterback in Super Bowl XX.

1985 CHICAGO BEARS
KEY STATS AND PLAYERS

Record: 15–1

Postseason: Won Super Bowl XX 46–10 over the New England Patriots

Richard Dent

Position: Defensive End

Age: 25

College: Tennessee State University

Gary Fencik

Position: Safety

Age: 31

College: Yale University

Wilber Marshall

Position: Linebacker

Age: 23

College: University of Florida

Mike Singletary

Position: Linebacker

Age: 27

College: Baylor University

1986
NEW YORK
GIANTS

There were defensive players who scared the living daylights out of quarterbacks before Lawrence Taylor.

None, however, did it quite like "L. T." The New York Giants' linebacker looked like a cat ready to pounce as he stood at the line of scrimmage waiting for the ball to be snapped.

Taylor was already known as the best outside linebacker of his generation by 1986. That year he teamed up with Carl Banks, Harry Carson, and Gary Reasons. They made one of the meanest, toughest, and fastest defenses in NFL history. The Giants didn't just beat teams. They destroyed them.

Lawrence Taylor of the New York Giants tackles the Philadelphia Eagles' quarterback in 1986.

New York had 59 sacks and forced 43 turnovers that season. And the Giants only got better as the season wore on. Taylor won the league's MVP award. That honor almost always goes to an offensive player. But he didn't give the voters much choice after racking up 20.5 sacks.

The Giants entered the playoffs with a 14–2 record. Then they allowed just one field goal in two playoff victories. That sent the Giants to their first Super Bowl. Superstar quarterback John Elway and the Denver Broncos awaited them in Super Bowl XXII. The Giants sacked Elway three times and tackled him for a safety in a 39–20 win.

L. T. and the Giants also would win Super Bowl XXV three years later. That time they shut down the high-powered Buffalo Bills 20–19. Many consider Super Bowl XXV to be the best Super Bowl ever played.

121

The total rushing yards allowed by the Giants in the 1986 playoffs. Each of the three opponents averaged more than 105 rushing yards per game during the regular season.

New York Giants linebacker Harry Carson sacks the St. Louis Cardinals' quarterback during a 1986 game.

1986 NEW YORK GIANTS
KEY STATS AND PLAYERS

Record: 14–2

Postseason: Won Super Bowl XXI 39–20 over the Denver Broncos

Carl Banks
Position: Linebacker
Age: 24
College: Michigan State University

Leonard Marshall
Position: Defensive End
Age: 25
College: Louisiana State University

Terry Kinard
Position: Free Safety
Age: 27
College: Clemson University

Lawrence Taylor
Position: Linebacker
Age: 27
College: University of North Carolina

2000
BALTIMORE RAVENS

Baltimore Ravens linebacker Ray Lewis began each game of his career with a dance. And in 2000, Lewis and the Ravens danced all over opposing offenses.

Offenses in that era were passing the ball like never before. But the Ravens were a throwback to old-time football. They hit. And they hit hard. And while Lewis earned NFL Defensive Player of the Year honors, he hardly did it alone.

Safety Rod Woodson was at the tail end of a Hall of Fame career. He picked off four passes and was second on the team with 67 tackles. Defensive lineman Rob Burnett collected 10.5 sacks. And nose tackle Tony Siragusa was a massive 330 pounds. He stuffed up the middle to shut down the run.

Baltimore Ravens defensive tackles Tony Siragusa (98) and Sam Adams (95) stop a Tennessee Titans player in 2000.

The Ravens allowed just 165 points that season. That was still the fewest points allowed in a 16-game regular season through 2012. Baltimore's defense needed to be stingy. After all, its offense had trouble scoring touchdowns. At one point the Ravens went three straight games without reaching the end zone.

By the end of the year, though, the offense was fine. The Ravens then steamrolled to their first Super Bowl. They gave up just one offensive touchdown in four playoff games. Baltimore ultimately crushed the New York Giants 35–7 in Super Bowl XXXV. The Ravens forced five turnovers in that game.

Lewis capped off his big year dancing in a rain of confetti as Super Bowl MVP.

2.7

The average number of yards per carry opponents gained against the 2000 Ravens. The NFL average that season was 4.1 yards per carry.

Linebacker Ray Lewis was the Baltimore Ravens' defensive leader during the 2000 season.

2000 BALTIMORE RAVENS
KEY STATS AND PLAYERS

Record: 12–4

Postseason: Won Super Bowl XXXV 35–7 over the New York Giants

Peter Boulware
Position: Linebacker
Age: 26
College: Florida State University

Ray Lewis
Position: Linebacker
Age: 25
College: University of Miami (Florida)

Duane Starks
Position: Cornerback
Age: 26
College: University of Miami (Florida)

Rod Woodson
Position: Safety
Age: 35
College: Purdue University

2002
TAMPA BAY BUCCANEERS

On the surface, Tampa Bay Buccaneers teammates Derrick Brooks and Warren Sapp could not have been more different. Brooks was a quiet, thoughtful middle linebacker who always seemed to find his way to the football. Sapp was a fast-talking defensive lineman who always seemed to find his way into trouble. Together, though, the two helped turn the lowly Buccaneers into champions.

Both players were selected in the first round of the 1995 NFL Draft. Together they gave Tampa Bay a new identity. The team had been one of the league's worst teams since it was founded in 1976. But Sapp and Brooks slowly changed all that.

Their hard work paid off in the 2002 season. Tampa Bay won its first Super Bowl behind a defense that made big play after big play.

Tampa Bay Buccaneers defensive tackle Warren Sapp celebrates during a 2002 win over the Cincinnati Bengals.

The Bucs led the NFL in fewest points allowed and fewest yards allowed. Brooks turned three of his five interceptions into touchdowns. And Sapp added 7.5 sacks. He even picked off two passes, which is rare for a player at his position.

Tampa Bay stormed to a 12–4 record during the regular season. Then the Bucs dominated the playoffs. They crushed the San Francisco 49ers and the Philadelphia Eagles to get to the Super Bowl.

The biggest game of the year turned into no contest. Tampa Bay beat the high-powered Oakland Raiders 48–21. The defense led the way. It scored three touchdowns off of interceptions. One of those interception-to-touchdown plays by Brooks sealed the victory in the fourth quarter.

172

The number of interception return yards by the Buccaneers in Super Bowl XXXVII, including 94 by Dwight Smith, who returned two picks for scores.

Tampa Bay Buccaneers safety John Lynch levels a St. Louis Rams wide receiver during a 2002 game.

2002 TAMPA BAY BUCCANEERS

KEY STATS AND PLAYERS

Record: 12–4

Postseason result: Won Super Bowl XXXVII 48–21 over the Oakland Raiders

Ronde Barber

Position: Cornerback

Age: 27

College: University of Virginia

Derrick Brooks

Position: Linebacker

Age: 29

College: Florida State University

Brian Kelly

Position: Cornerback

Age: 26

College: University of Southern California

Warren Sapp

Position: Defensive Tackle

Age: 30

College: University of Miami (Florida)

2008
PITTSBURGH STEELERS

James Harrison and Troy Polamalu were the faces of the 2008 Pittsburgh Steelers' defense. Yet they looked quite different. Linebacker Harrison had no hair and a mean streak. Meanwhile safety Polamalu had long curly hair that overflowed from his helmet, and he was almost always smiling. Together the pair of opposites gave the 2008 Steelers a one-two punch that led the team to a record sixth Super Bowl title.

Harrison chased after quarterbacks. He recorded 16 tackles that year. Polamalu chased after passes. He collected seven interceptions. They were the backbone of a defense that led the NFL in fewest yards allowed. That's something the Steelers did five times between 2004 and 2012.

Pittsburgh Steelers safety Troy Polamalu gets into pass coverage in the snow against the Cincinnati Bengals in 2008.

Polamalu and Harrison were at their best in the 2008 playoffs.

Polamalu returned an interception 40 yards for a touchdown in the conference championship game. Then Harrison one-upped that in Super Bowl XLV against the Arizona Cardinals.

The Cardinals were getting ready to score late in the first half. That's when Harrison picked off quarterback Kurt Warner. The 242-pound Harrison then chugged 100 yards for a score. It was one of the biggest plays in Super Bowl history. Instead of falling behind at the half, the Steelers were able to take a 17–7 lead.

The Cardinals rallied and had one last chance. But Pittsburgh linebacker LaMarr Woodley came up with a big sack that ended the game and let the Steelers celebrate another championship.

157

The number of passing yards per game the Steelers allowed in 2008, the lowest in the NFL. That was 23 yards less per game than the second-ranked Baltimore Ravens.

Pittsburgh Steelers linebacker James Harrison strips the New England Patriots' quarterback during a 2008 game.

2008 PITTSBURGH STEELERS
KEY STATS AND PLAYERS

Record: 12–4

Postseason: Won Super Bowl XLV 27–23 over the Arizona Cardinals

James Farrior
Position: Linebacker
Age: 33
College: University of Virginia

James Harrison
Position: Linebacker
Age: 30
College: Kent State University

Troy Polamalu
Position: Safety
Age: 27
College: University of Southern California

LaMarr Woodley
Position: Linebacker
Age: 24
College: University of Michigan

SHAPING THE GAME

Defense in football has changed over the years. Here are some of the defensive schemes that have revolutionized the NFL.

Nickel Defense – A nickel defense uses five defensive backs instead of the usual four. The fifth defensive back is called the "nickel back," kind of like how a nickel is worth five pennies. The nickel defense often is used when the opposing offense is likely to pass the ball. It became popular during the 1970s when passing became more common.

Zone Blitz – A blitz is when the defense sends extra players to chase after the quarterback. A zone blitz is a little trickier. In a zone blitz, some players will race after the quarterback while other players will drop back into pass coverage. The goal is to not let the quarterback know which players are coming after him.

Zone Defense – In this scheme, defenders cover an area of the field instead of a specific player, which is called man defense. They then cover any offensive player who comes into their area. Zone defense is supposed to make it harder for quarterbacks to complete passes, because it makes them think longer before they throw the ball. Most NFL teams switch between zone and man defenses during the game.

4–3 Defense – This scheme is called the 4–3 because it has four defensive linemen and three linebackers near the line of scrimmage. Former Dallas Cowboys coach Tom Landry invented it when he was a defensive coach for the New York Giants in the 1950s. In this scheme, the defense gets rid of the nose tackle and instead uses a middle linebacker. A middle linebacker lines up off the line of scrimmage. He has more freedom than a defensive lineman to go tackle the player with the ball.

GLOSSARY

draft
A system used by professional sports leagues to select new players in order to spread incoming talent among all teams. The NFL Draft is held each April.

dynasty
A team that wins several titles over a short period of time.

founded
Began from scratch.

Pro Bowl
An annual All-Star game that takes place the week before the Super Bowl.

sack
When a quarterback is tackled before he can pass the ball.

scheme
A system of offense or defense.

stingy
Not giving much away.

turnover
Any time the defense takes the ball away from the offense, whether it's a fumble or an interception.

FOR MORE INFORMATION

Further Readings

Gramling, Gary. *Sports Illustrated Kids 1st and 10: Top 10 Lists of Everything in Football*. New York: Sports Illustrated, 2011.

Jacobs, Greg. *The Everything Kids Football Book, Third Edition*. New York: F+W Media, 2012.

Polzer, Tim. *NFL Reader: Defense*. New York: Scholastic Inc., 2011.

Web Links

To learn more about the NFL's best defenses, visit ABDO Publishing Company online at **www.abdopublishing.com**. Web sites about the NFL's best defenses are featured on our Book Links page. These links are routinely monitored and updated to provide the most current information available.

INDEX

ABOUT THE AUTHOR

Will Graves got hooked on football when he was eight years old, watching the Washington Redskins win their first Super Bowl. He's covered sports since 1996, and he joined the Associated Press in 2005. He currently works in Pittsburgh, Pennsylvania, where he writes about the Pittsburgh Steelers but still finds time to cheer on the Redskins every Sunday.